THE INDIAN TRIBES
OF CANADA

A CHIPEWYAN INDIAN

THE INDIAN TRIBES
OF CANADA

BY
EILEEN JENNESS

McGRAW-HILL RYERSON LIMITED

Toronto   Montreal   New York   London   Sydney
Johannesburg   Mexico   Panama   Düsseldorf   Singapore
Sao Paulo   Kuala Lumpur   New Delhi

ACKNOWLEDGMENT

THE author and publishers gratefully acknowledge the courtesy of the National Museum of Canada in lending the plates and cuts for the illustrations and maps in this book. The author wishes also to acknowledge with thanks the assistance of her husband, Diamond Jenness, from whose volume "The Indians of Canada" she has derived her material; and the kindness of M. Paul Coze, the well-known French artist, in permitting the reproduction of his painting "A Chipewyan Indian" as a frontispiece.

CONTENTS

THE INDIAN TRIBES
OF CANADA

CHAPTER I

INTRODUCTION

ON a clear day one may stand on the extreme northwest point of America, in the little village of Wales, and glimpse on the far horizon the grey outline of East Cape, on the Asiatic shore. Over this narrow fifty-mile strait that separates the two continents scientists believe the earliest Indians made their way into America. The first-comers, fifteen thousand or twenty thousand years ago, were, perhaps, but a few scattered bands who crossed the narrow neck of water in search of better hunting-grounds and new homes where they could wander unmolested by enemies. Miles and miles of virgin country teeming with fish and game must have seemed to these wandering, harassed bands a veritable paradise. Probably they first ascended the wide valley of the Yukon River, struggled across the great barrier of mountains, and, reaching the valley of the Mackenzie River, made their way along the eastern foothills of the Rockies through what we now call Alberta. Centuries went by, and as the population increased and the migrations from Asia continued, the tribes moved farther and farther south until finally both North and South America were overrun. The last migrants from Asia, the Eskimo, arrived perhaps not more than three thousand or four thousand years ago; they are even to-day distinct from the Indians in their appearance and customs, and some of their kinsmen still linger on the Siberian shore.

The land to which the nomadic groups came differed greatly from their old homes. Canada is a country divided naturally into very marked geographic regions. There is the indented Pacific coast-line with its islands and fiords; the Cordillera and its plateaus; the wide, rolling central prairies; the wooded highlands of Ontario, Quebec and the Maritime Provinces; and the green fertile basin of southeastern Ontario and its extension along the St. Lawrence valley. Each of these regions has its own soil, its own vegetation, and its own fish and game. It was thus natural that the Indians should have gradually split

2

into groups, composed of many different tribes, that restricted themselves to these geographic areas. Each group adapted itself to its new environment, and its individual tribes, even when they retained their separate languages, acquired the same general customs and the same broad manner of life. So, although there are still more than fifty tribes scattered from the Atlantic to the Pacific and from the Arctic to the boundary of the United States, we can arrange them conveniently into but seven geographic groups:

1. *Algonkian Tribes of the Eastern Woodlands.* The Micmac Indians dwelling in Nova Scotia; the Malecite of New Brunswick; the Montagnais of Eastern Quebec; the Naskapi of the Labrador peninsula; the Algonkin [1] between the Ottawa River and the St. Maurice; the Ojibwa of northern Ontario; the Cree from James Bay westward to the prairies; and, finally, the extinct tribe of Beothuk Indians in Newfoundland.

2. *Iroquoian Tribes of the Eastern Woodlands.* The Five Nations of the Iroquois

---

[1] Algonkin should be carefully distinguished from Algonkian. The Algonkin is only one of many tribes who speak the Algonkian language; the term "Algonkian peoples" covers all these tribes, Ojibwa, Cree, Algonkin, etc. Similarly distinguish Iroquois from Iroquoian.

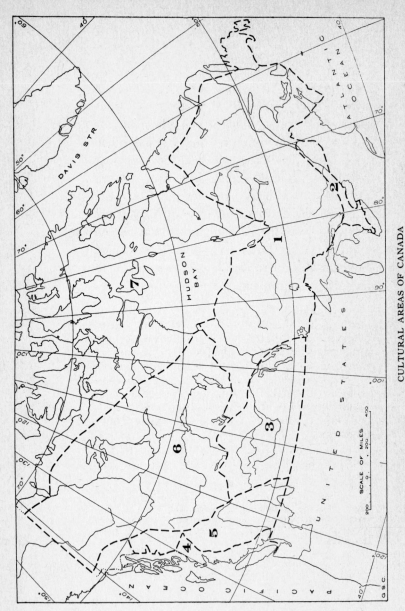

CULTURAL AREAS OF CANADA

1. Algonkian tribes of the eastern woodlands; 2. The Iroquoians; 3. Plains' tribes; 4. Tribes of the Pacific coast; 5. Plateau tribes of British Columbia; 6. Tribes of the Mackenzie and Yukon basins; 7. The Eskimo.

(Seneca, Oneida, Onondaga, Cayuga, and Mohawk) who lived south of the St. Lawrence from the Richelieu River to Lake Erie; the Huron of the Lake Simcoe area; and the now extinct Tobacco and Neutral tribes of the Niagara Peninsula.

3. *The Plains' Indians.* The Blackfoot; the Sarcee; the Assiniboine or Stonies; and, after the introduction of horses, a branch of the Cree.

4. *The Pacific Coast Indians.* The Tlinkit of southwest Alaska who encroached on what is now British Columbia; the Tsimshian of the Nass and Skeena Rivers; the Haida of Queen Charlotte Islands; the Bella Bella from Douglas Channel to Rivers Inlet; the Bella Coola of Bella Coola Inlet and River; the Kwakiutl on the east coast of Vancouver Island; the Nootka on the west coast of the same island; and the Salish Indians along its southeast coast and around the mouth of the Fraser River.

5. *The Plateau Indians of British Columbia.* The Interior Salish; the Kootenay; the Chilcotin of the Chilco River district; the Carrier along the northern line of the Canadian National Railway; the extinct Tsetsaut tribe at the head of Portland Canal; the Tahltan on the Stikine River; and the Tagish of the Atlin Lake district.

6. *The Mackenzie and Yukon River Indians.* The Sekani at the head of the Peace River; the Beaver lower down its course; the Chipewyan who roamed between Hudson Bay, the Athabaska River, and Great Slave Lake; the Yellow-Knives, northeast of Great Slave Lake; the

Dog-Rib between Great Slave and Great Bear Lakes; the Slave on the Mackenzie River from Great Slave Lake almost to Norman; the Hare from Norman to the ramparts of the Mackenzie River; the Loucheux or Kutchin of the Peel River; and the little-known Nahani tribes on the eastern slopes of the Rocky Mountains from the Liard River to the Arctic Circle.

7. *The Eskimo* of the Arctic coast, the shores of Hudson Bay, and the Labrador peninsula.

When Columbus, in 1492, landed his mutineering crew in the West Indies, he thought himself in the Indies of southeastern Asia, and called the people of the New World "Indians." The misnomer has remained unchanged. All the native tribes of Canada (with the exception of the Eskimo), though they may differ from one another as widely as Italians from Englishmen, and though they often understand not a word of one another's languages (there are eleven different languages and many distinct dialects), are one and all called "Indians."

When the early explorers first set foot on Canadian soil, they still hoped to find an "Indies" rich in spices and precious stones, and peoples clad in silks and Oriental embroideries, but they, too, found only vast stretches of

primæval forest and primitive natives still
living in an age of stone, ignorant even of the
use of iron. Most of the inhabitants of the
Dominion lived entirely by hunting and fishing; a few tribes cultivated the ground, but to
a very limited extent, as the only native cereal
was corn, the only vegetables squashes and
beans. The homes of the natives were rude
shelters of bark or skin: their principal tools
were knives and axes made from stone; their
few household utensils were crudely shaped
from wood, stone, bone or horn, and in some
districts rough pottery; and their sole domes-
ticated animal was the dog. In no respect,
except that they were human beings, did they
resemble the civilized peoples of the Malay
Archipelago, or the subjects of the magnificent
Kublai Khan.[1]

In appearance they differed from any people
the Europeans had ever seen. For want of
a better name, the explorers described them as
"red" Indians, but this term also was mis-
leading. The skin of the Indian is seldom red,

---

[1] The great Mongol ruler (1260-1295) whose empire
extended from China to the boundaries of Austria. The
splendour of his court was described by the Venetian
traveller, Marco Polo.

7

SOME BASIC ABORIGINAL STONE TOOLS
Knife, adze, hammer, drill, and scraper

but is rather some shade of brown, grading from the pale creamish-yellow of the Eskimo, through shades of yellowish-brown, to an occasional deep-brown tinged with red. The eyes range in colour from medium to dark brown, and often slant a little, though not as much as in the Chinese and Japanese; the hair is black and lank; the face is wider, and the cheek bones more prominent than among Europeans; and the body and limbs are well-proportioned, although the feet and hands are often somewhat small. The stature varies in different regions: the Indians east of the Rocky Mountains, and some of the Eskimo, are of medium height, with here and there a tendency to tallness, especially among the Iroquois, whereas in British Columbia most of the natives are short, thick-set, and rather squat. The Eskimo differ from the Indians in many respects; probably they inherit some of the same racial blood, but they should be regarded as a special type, that has changed considerably owing to the severe climate of the Arctic and the harsh diet its inhabitants endure.

Chapter II

ALGONKIAN TRIBES OF THE EASTERN WOODLANDS

B Y the time Jacques Cartier had ascended the St. Lawrence River to "Mont Real," and viewed from its summit only vast stretches of unbroken forest and encampments of savages dotting the shore-line of the rivers, all hope of finding in Canada anything but unexplored territory and strange native tribes had vanished from the explorers' minds.

The St. Lawrence River, with its tributary the Ottawa, was in those days the dividing line between two large groups of Indians destined later to play an important rôle in the history of Canada. To the south were agricultural peoples, each of whom spoke some dialect of the Iroquoian language. North of these rivers, and in the Maritime Provinces, were tribes of wandering hunters who practised little or no agriculture, and who all spoke dialects of the wide-spread Algonkian language. At that time Eastern Canada was extremely rich in land and sea animals.

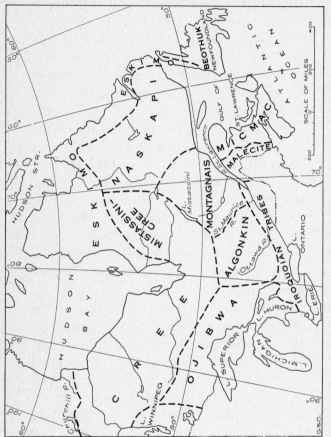

APPROXIMATE DISTRIBUTION OF THE EASTERN ALGONKIAN TRIBES IN 1525 A.D.

The Atlantic coast teemed with salmon that migrated up the rivers and creeks to spawn at the headwaters; cod, seals and even walruses abounded in the Gulf of St. Lawrence; bears, moose, caribou, deer, rabbits and numerous species of wild fowl tenanted the forests, or haunted the margins of the innumerable lakes. Except in unusually severe winters the Indian, despite his primitive weapons, had not that grim fear of starvation that so often pursued him after the coming of the white man. He was trained from childhood to observe Nature in all her moods. He knew the haunts and feeding-grounds of the animals in his district, knew the habits of the fish that bred in the lakes or migrated up the rivers and streams from the sea, and he stored away in his mind, without the aid of books, the "virtue" of every plant and tree. Indeed, his life depended upon this self-taught knowledge, for he had no conception of the great world that lay without, and could not import food or clothing, could not dress lumber or stone, or make bricks to build a house. Only from the woods and waters round him, and through his own exertions, could he obtain food and

12

clothing and a shelter to protect his family. Yet he had a quick intelligence, and so long as the animals roved the forests in undiminished numbers, so long as the fish abounded in the lakes and streams, and the forests were untouched by fire, he generally succeeded in providing his family with the few demands of daily life.

All the Algonkian tribes, though they differed in many ways one from another, lived this roving hunters' life. There were no roads in the country, no bridges spanning the rivers. The numerous waterways were the highways, and the birch-bark canoe the chief means of transportation during the greater part of the year. The natives were highly skilled in the making and handling of the canoe, and the early white explorers and fur-traders found both the boatmen and their craft indispensable for navigating the swift rivers of the country. It was the birch-bark canoe, indeed, that in later days provided the model for the cedar and bass-wood canoes used everywhere throughout Canada at the present time. Sometimes the Indians of the Maritimes made a skin-boat by covering a crude

OJIBWA INDIAN WOMEN IN A BIRCH-BARK CANOE

frame with moose-skin, but they used it only to travel down to the coast in the early spring, and discarded it at the end of the trip.

Algonkian families were continually moving to new fishing and hunting grounds, according to the changes in the seasons. Of all their game animals the most important was the moose, for they ate its flesh, clothed themselves with its skin, made tools from its bones, and thread from its sinews. Its skin provided also bedding and rugs for the wigwams. The Indians hunted the moose mainly during the winter months, when they hunted also caribou, deer and smaller game. In spring they laid aside their snowshoes, and with their entire families moved to the mouths of creeks and rivers to fish for salmon; or else they travelled down to the seashore to gather shellfish and eels, and to hunt the seals that were so abundant in the Gulf of St. Lawrence. The westernmost tribe, however, the Ojibwa of Northern Ontario, pitched their camps at this season in the maple groves, where they made large quantities of maple syrup and sugar, native products that are to-day so popular with white people.

15

When travelling overland, all the members of a family helped with the moving, and loaded on their backs the belongings of the camp. They wrapped their goods in squares of moose-skin, or packed them into birch-bark or splint hampers, which they carried with the aid of a tump-line drawn across the forehead, and sometimes an extra strap across the chest and arms. In winter they used toboggans (an Indian invention) when travelling over the deep snow. In many parts of Canada the natives trained their dogs to take a share of the load; but, except among the Eskimo and Plains' tribes, whose dogs were of a larger and stronger breed, the main burden of packing [1] always fell on the natives themselves.

Throughout the summer, the main diet was fish, large quantities of which were dried and stored in caches for seasons of scarcity. The women gathered wild fruits and berries, and many varieties of roots and nuts. If the season were favourable, they dried part of the harvest and stored it away for the winter when fresh fruit was no longer available. The wild

---

[1] A term of the early fur-traders meaning to carry goods on the back in a roll or "pack."

rice that grows abundantly in eastern Canada round the shores of many lakes makes an excellent food, but only the Ojibwa collected it and used it to supplement their diet of berries, fish and meat.

Owing to their migratory existence, the Algonkian tribes could build only imperfect and temporary dwellings. They chose for their camping-grounds dry, sandy sites that were close to water and fuel, preferably near a hill-side from which they could scan the neighbouring landscape. Just as birch-bark was essential for their baskets and canoes, so it was for their homes. Over a rectangular, conical, or beehive framework of poles, they overlapped sheets of bark until the structure was entirely enclosed. The fireplace was on the ground in the centre, the chimney merely a hole in the roof through which the smoke made its way. Instead of birch-bark for the cover of their wigwams the Ojibwa of the Great Lakes region sometimes used strips of matting made from rushes, while the more northern tribes of Ontario and Quebec, in whose territory large birch trees were scarce, used skins. All tribes alike strewed

17

fir boughs around the walls inside the dwelling, and, if they intended to occupy it for some time, covered the boughs with rush mats. As many as two or three families often huddled inside one small shelter, sleeping on the boughs or mats with no extra wraps whatever, or covered by their skin cloaks.

During the warm Eastern Woodland summer, the Indian hunter discarded all his clothing except his breech-cloth and soft hide moccasins; the women wore at all seasons a long skin dress that fell to the moccasins. In winter the women added short leggings that fastened below the knee, while the men had longer leggings that reached the thigh, and a shirt that barely overlapped the leggings. Both sexes wore mittens and caps, and, in very cold weather, heavy robes that served also as bed coverings. The affluent Indian had extra ceremonial garments—including a bizarre head-dress mounted with dyed feathers—that were gaudily painted, or embroidered with moose-hair or porcupine quills. Moose-hide supplied the material for all the clothing except the robe and cap, which were generally

Photo by T. C. Weston

TWO TYPES OF OJIBWA BIRCH-BARK LODGES

of beaver or other small skins. Both men and women delighted in necklets and bracelets, and even ear and nose pendants. Some tattooed their faces and bodies, but in most tribes they preferred the less permanent decoration given by various paints.

The organization of each tribe was fairly simple, for it rested upon the family, and the family, as among Europeans, consisted of a man, his wife, and their children. To assist one another in obtaining food, several families that were closely related joined together to form a band. Wherever a number of these bands spoke the same language and had the same customs, they constituted a "tribe"; yet throughout the woodlands of eastern Canada the tribe was very indefinite, the only clear political unit being the band. Each band had its leader, who owed his position to his personality alone, not to any election. The band did not divide up its territory among the individual families, but retained it as the property of the whole group, and decided year by year in council meetings where each family should fish and hunt. There was no military training whatever among the Algonkians, no thought of war for the acquisition of new territory; the only reason for war was self-protection, or the desire for revenge. Likewise, there were no police or formal ways of keeping law and order. The censure of public opinion was generally sufficient to prevent wrong-doing, and a council of the hunters could prescribe death for grave offences such as murder or witchcraft. Strangers had no rights whatever; all were considered as enemies, and any native might rob or kill an "outsider" without fear of punishment.

Romance played but a small part in the lives of these migratory tribes, as the constant search for food and clothing left little time for the gentler emotions. As soon as boys and girls left childhood they ceased to play together, the boys following the men on their hunting and fishing expeditions, the girls sewing, cooking and attending to the many duties that fell to the lot of the women. The parents usually arranged betrothals, often when the children were very young, but marriage did not take place until the girls were about fourteen or fifteen years of age, the men nineteen or twenty. In some tribes the only formal procedure was, that the youth should hunt with his bride's parents during the first year, or until the first child was born, giving all the proceeds of his hunting and fishing to his father- and mother-in-law; thereafter the young couple could separate from the parents, and build their own wigwam wherever they wished. A husband had full control over his wife, but either could divorce the other at will and remarry as long as they remained childless; once children had been born to them, they seldom, if ever, separated.

The nomadic life of the Algonkians, and their complete ignorance of infant hygiene, led to a very high death-rate among the children. Those that survived had a care-free existence; they were always treated with kindness and affection by parents and relatives, and permitted an unrestricted life seldom enjoyed by white boys and girls. There were, of course, no schools, no formal education of any kind. The children learned all they needed to know through a quick observation of nature, and through making and performing as pastimes the things they would need to do in later years. The boys made bows and arrows, canoes and toboggans; and they played at hunting and fishing. The little girls, as part of their play, learned to sew, to cook, to make bark vessels, and to embroider skin and bark with moose-hair or porcupine quills. Ethically there was no systematic training, but in the evenings around the camp-fires the old people gathered the children together and told them stories of olden times, of brave deeds, the obedience of children to their elders, the generosity of a chief to his people, and many such tales with the moral hidden in the atmosphere of romance. The children seldom received whippings or rough blows, but were reprimanded with the same subtlety, in the presence of their relatives around the evening fire.

There were many occasions when the Indians met together and indulged in feasts and social gatherings. Seasonal events of nature, such as the first running of the maple sap, the ripening of berries, and the migration of the salmon, led to many festivals, which the Indians enjoyed the more because of their hard labour at other times of the year. Their love of gambling amounted almost to a passion,

CAMP OF A NASKAPI FAMILY

Photo by F. W. Waugh.

and there were many games, trivial in themselves, in which they could easily divest themselves of all their belongings. Archery was a favourite pastime, and different kinds of athletics, such as wrestling and running, were popular amongst the men and boys. The game of lacrosse originated amongst these eastern people, and in olden days created almost "league" enthusiasm. All the Indians loved to dance, but there was no similarity between their individual gymnastic step-dances and our modern rhythmic dancing. Rattles and drums constituted their sole musical instruments, and these were seldom used except for dances or religious ceremonies. Singing, too, was but the accompaniment of a ceremony, seldom a spontaneous outburst of music.

In spite of the so-called paganism of the Algonkians, who were the first Indians to be visited by the missionaries, they nevertheless had a very real religious life of their own, and their beliefs were so deep-seated that, even after they embraced the Christian faith, their own remained rooted beneath the surface of the new. From their pagan religion they sought help and guidance in this present life

alone; they considered death but the passing
on of the soul to another world about which
they knew too little to question. So they
fasted and prayed for purely earthly blessings,
for health and happiness, success in hunting,
and children to carry on their race.

In a vague way every Indian acknowledged
the presence of a Great Spirit, who, though
he may not have created the earth, at least
presided over it; he believed also in many
lesser deities or spirits, and propitiated
them continually with sacrifices, especially of
tobacco. He thought that everything in
nature, fish, animals, flowers, rocks, was
imbued with life and with a soul similar to
man's, and from this belief he developed many
strict regulations about hunting, fishing, and
the routine of daily life. These rules, taught
from infancy, gave him a general idea of what
was considered right and wrong. Just as he
propitiated his deities, so he made sacrifices to
the souls of animals and fish which he killed,
lest they should be offended and disappear
altogether from the country.

Medicine-men played an important rôle in
the religious life. They were individuals,

usually highly emotional, who, by long fasting
and seclusion in their youth, claimed to have
received visions and messages from the spirit
world that gave them power to mediate
between the Indians and the spirits. As a rule
these medicine-men were perfectly sincere, and
were quite convinced that the spirits were
responsible for their actions, even when these
were no more than mere conjuring or sleight-
of-hand tricks; sometimes, however, they
abused their gifts and practised witchcraft to
harm their countrymen. Besides their psychic
powers they made use of medicinal herbs and
ointments, which they gathered from the
woods; and where these had not the necessary
healing properties, mental suggestion often
completed the cure.

Amongst all the Eastern Indians the medicine-men employed for their divinations the
shaking-lodge, a circle of sticks about six feet
high "sheeted" in with layers of birch-bark.
There was no door; the medicine-man lifted
one of the layers of bark, crawled inside, and
drew the bark into place again. Once inside,
he called on various spirits to tell him why a
certain man was ill, where the Indians could

find abundant game, and other requests that had been made to him beforehand by his people. The lodge began to shake violently, apparently signifying the presence of the spirits whom the medicine-man seemed to be questioning inside the enclosure. So firmly did the Indians believe in the power of the shaking-lodge that even to-day, in remote districts, they use them for communing with the other world. But the medicine-man lost much of his influence and prestige when smallpox and other virulent diseases, brought in by Europeans, carried away the Indians by hundreds, and his shaking-lodge and other mystical remedies proved powerless in the face of such deadly ailments.

Chapter III

THE IROQUOIANS

JUST as the use of birch-bark, the hunting of the moose, and a simple form of government, stand out boldly from the Algonkian picture, so amongst the Iroquoian tribes, living close by and yet differing so widely from their neighbours, agriculture, military training, and a complex form of government will stamp themselves upon our memory. The St. Lawrence River, its tributary, the Ottawa, and an imaginary line drawn from Ottawa to Lake Simcoe, formed the dividing line between the ever-shifting camps of the Algonkian tribes and the semi-permanent farms of the Iroquoians. The Huron, the Tobacco, and the Neutral nations (all of whom were destroyed by the Iroquois proper in the 17th century), inhabited the southern part of Ontario; and the Five Nations of the Iroquois occupied the territory south of the Great Lakes and the St. Lawrence, as far east as Lake Champlain. So important a part did agriculture play in the lives of these Indians, that the sites for their

29

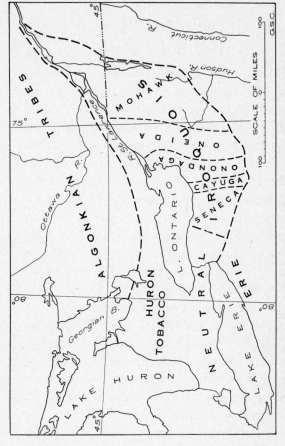

APPROXIMATE DISTRIBUTION OF THE IROQUOIAN TRIBES IN 1525 A.D.

Based partly on map in Beauchamp, W.M., "A History of the New York Iroquois," New York State Museum, Bull. 78. The boundaries between the Huron, Tobacco and Neutral nations, and what tribe or tribes controlled the north shore of the St. Lawrence River, are not known.

encampments were chosen mainly with a view to the fertility of the soil. Agriculture was their greatest strength, providing them with food right at their doors against times when fish and game were scarce; yet it also proved a source of weakness, for any sudden or unexpected destruction of their crops meant a complete cutting-off of most of their year's food supply.

The land was largely covered with forest, and required a vast amount of work before the seed could be put into the ground. To clear their fields, which extended over many acres, the men burned the trees around the base, and chipped away the charcoal with their stone axes until they fell; two or three years later, whatever stumps remained they rooted out with digging sticks and shell-bladed hoes. The work of the "farm" then became the responsibility of the women, on whose shoulders fell all the labour of tilling, planting, weeding and harvesting. Their principal crop was corn, which they planted in small mounds of earth set up a few feet apart; between the hillocks they sowed also the seed of squash, sunflowers (from which they made an oil),

and several varieties of beans. Besides their
vegetables, they grew large quantities of
tobacco, which they smoked in their pipes of
clay or soapstone, and traded extensively with
non-agricultural neighbours. The same corn
and tobacco fields were cultivated continuously
for from ten to fifteen years, but yielded
poorer and poorer harvests, for the Indians
had no knowledge of fertilization or rotation
of crops. This necessitated their moving to
new lands before the soil became utterly
exhausted. So, toward the last years of their
stay in one village, they chose the location for
their next encampment, and cleared the adjoin-
ing land for the gardens; when they moved
to their new homes, they were able to plant at
once, without the loss of a single harvest.

Tending the fields during the greater part
of the year kept the women at home, and necessitated dwellings more comfortable and permanent than the wigwams hastily built by
their roving Algonkian neighbours. Champlain has given us a graphic picture of their
"long-houses" in his description of the Huron:

"Their cabins are a kind of arbour or bower,
covered with bark, approximately fifty or sixty

CORN CULTIVATION AMONG THE HURONS

(From J. F. Lafitau, *Mœurs des Sauvages Amériquains*, Paris, 1724)

yards long by twelve wide, with a passage ten or twelve feet broad down the middle from one end to the other. Along each side runs a bench four feet above the ground, where the inmates sleep in summer to avoid the innumerable fleas. In winter they sleep close to the fire on mats, underneath the benches where it is warmer; and they fill the hut with a supply of dry wood to burn at that season. A space is left at one end of the cabin for storing their maize, which they place in large bark barrels in the middle of the floor; and boards suspended overhead preserve their clothing, food and other things from the numerous mice. There will be a dozen fires to each cabin, making two dozen families. The smoke circulates at will, causing much eye trouble, to which the natives are so subject that many become blind in their old age. For there is no window in the cabin, no opening except a place in the roof where the smoke finds an outlet."

The Iroquoians wore very much the same type of skin garments as the Algonkians, and as freely discarded them when the weather became warm. Dressing the skins, and making the clothing for all the members of the "long-house," made heavy demands upon the time of the women, for their only tailoring tools were scrapers of bone and stone, knives of stone or copper, bodkins to punch holes,

34

bone needles of various sizes, and thread of twisted sinew.

The semi-sedentary life their agricultural existence allowed gave these tribes an opportunity to develop systems of government far higher than any found elsewhere in Canada, except on the Pacific Coast. They were the only systems in which the women played a really important rôle, and this in spite of the fact that they held an inferior position to the men, and were forced to labour in the fields and perform all the drudgery in the village. The Iroquois proper, or the Five Nations, as they are commonly called, were exceptionally strong and well organized, and more than a match for the combined Hurons and Algonkians with whom they were at war when the Europeans established their first settlements on the St. Lawrence. The French soon realized the grave mistake Champlain had made in taking sides against the Iroquois, and tried again and again to regain their confidence; but the seeds of distrust had been too deeply sown, and most of the natives refused to be drawn into an alliance.

We know but little of the details of govern-

ment among the Huron, Tobacco, and Neutral
Nations, because they were destroyed by the
Iroquois in the 17th century. Among the
latter, each of the five "nations" was divided
into four or more clans, like the clans in the
Highland glens; and the score or more families
that lived in one house generally belonged to
the same clan. A man did not belong to his
father's clan, but to his mother's, because the
Iroquois, unlike ourselves, traced their descent
through their mothers, not through their
fathers. A man could not marry a woman
who belonged to the same clan as himself, but
married an outside woman and lived in her
home as a kind of guest. Thus, it was really
the women who owned the long-houses and
their furniture, although the men built them.
In practice, the women of each clan selected
one of their number as "matron," and she
governed all the inmates of her house, and of
other houses occupied by the same clan.

Shortly after America was discovered the
Iroquois united their five tribes, Mohawk,
Oneida, Onondaga, Cayuga and Seneca, into
a confederacy called the "League of the Five
Nations," which became the "Six Nations,"

MODEL OF AN IROQUOIS "LONG HOUSE" OF BARK

In the Rochester Municipal Museum.

about 1722, when the Tuscarora Indians of Carolina moved northward and joined them. This league was governed by a council composed of fifty sachems, or chiefs, selected from certain clans to hold office for life. Whenever a clan's representative died, the "matron" of that clan selected a new chief, and the council approved or disapproved her choice; if the new chief proved unworthy of his position, the "matron" had the power to depose him, and to choose another. The council assembled three or four times a year to arbitrate disputes, to receive delegates from other tribes, and to decide whether the nations should go to war or remain at peace.

These fifty chiefs, however, were purely civil chiefs; they gained their rank not from outstanding character or prowess in war, but because they were born in certain clans, and selected by the "matrons" of those clans. It was inevitable that there should arise also a group of warrior chiefs, for Iroquois boys were trained to warfare almost from the time they could walk, and the division of labour that left agriculture in the hands of the women gave the men and boys ample time for raids

38

and forays. Certain outstanding individuals
naturally became the leaders in these raids,
and when they added diplomacy to daring they
attained greater influence and more promi-
nence than the civil chiefs themselves. But
this double set of chiefs eventually proved a
stumbling-block, for when the Iroquois came
to be lined up against European forces accus-
tomed to strict discipline and a single com-
mand, their very lack of unity hindered their
striking a decisive blow.

In war they sometimes treated their prisoners cruelly, torturing even women and children; but they spared the majority of their
captives, and even absorbed them into their
nations with full rights of citizenship. In
their domestic life they were a kindly and
affectionate people, full of sympathy for
friends and relatives in distress, and exceedingly fond of their children. Law and order
were made the responsibility of each village,
which had to pay compensation, usually in
wampum beads, for every offence committed
by one of its members. Theft, so common
amongst whites, was very rare, for such personal property as tools and household articles

were of little value, and food was always shared without question with needier neighbours. The only objects open to theft were the strings of wampum, used both as money and as ornaments; but so public-spirited were the Iroquois, and so little did they value the accumulation of mere wealth, that even these were seldom stolen. The whole structure of their society was democratic, and though there were both civil chiefs and warrior chiefs, these differed in no way, either in dress or in aloofness, from the common people.

The Iroquois held broadly the same religious beliefs as the Algonkians, though their ideas about the supernatural world were a little more definite. They were the only Indians who believed in two Great Spirits, one good and one evil, always in conflict with one another; and their folk-tales contain many episodes about these two warring deities, and about the havoc and good each wrought in turn throughout the world. Like all their neighbours, the Iroquois had also their medicine-men who pretended to foresee the future and to cure diseases through the help of the spirit world.

Of all the natives of Eastern Canada the

40

The Iroquoians

Five Nations of the Iroquois alone seem to have possessed the seeds of greatness. They were laying the foundation stones of a great empire to stretch from the Atlantic Ocean to the western margins of the Great Lakes. They had anchored themselves to the soil with agriculture, established a kind of federal government, evolved with wampum beads a currency system that stimulated trade, and organized their man - power for aggressive warfare against the surrounding Algonkian tribes and their own kinsmen the Huron. However, European colonists still better organized, and with more efficient weapons, arrested their progress and caused their incipient empire to collapse.

Chapter IV

INDIANS OF THE PLAINS

WHEN the coureurs-de-bois had tasted the spoils of the fur-trade among each tribe in succession from the Atlantic to the head-waters of the Ottawa River, their adventurous spirit drove them still further afield to exploit the unknown tribes of the west. Their highways were the rivers and lakes, their craft the Indian birch-bark canoe, and their knowledge of the Algonkian language that prevailed all the way from the eastern seacoast to the prairies, aided them greatly in their trade with the natives. But the prairies, with their lack of fur-bearing animals, their miles of grassland broken only by occasional lakes and rivers, and their Indians speaking unknown tongues, provided little attraction for these earliest fur-traders. So they skirted their borders along the waterways in the north of Manitoba and Saskatchewan, where a well-wooded country, and Cree Indians speaking the same dialect as their kinsmen in Ontario and Quebec, offered them familiar surroundings and filled their

42

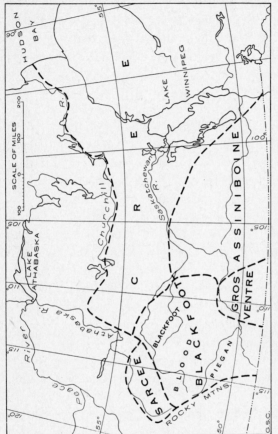

APPROXIMATE DISTRIBUTION OF THE PLAINS' TRIBES IN 1725 A.D.

canoes with furs. Thus, trading-posts were dotted throughout the whole northern district long before the prairies were explored and settled. Meanwhile, the spread of the horse northward from Mexico, and the introduction of firearms from the Mississippi valley and from Hudson Bay, revolutionized the whole life of the Plains' Indians. So it is well to have a picture of them in their pre-white days, when their very primitiveness brought safety to themselves and to the buffalo that was the nucleus and mainstay of their lives.

These nomads of the prairies consisted of three distinct tribes: the Blackfoot, who roamed over southern Alberta and southern Saskatchewan; the Sarcee, a much smaller tribe living north of the Blackfoot; and the Assiniboine, who occupied the prairie parts of Manitoba and extended into northern Saskatchewan. As the three tribes spoke mutually unintelligible languages, they developed a system of communicating and trading by signs; and one may still see an old Blackfoot Indian, ignorant of any language but his own, conversing by gestures with a visitor from another tribe.

TWO ASSINIBOINE INDIANS RUNNING A BUFFALO

From a painting by Paul Kane.

In prehistoric days these prairie Indians lived a quiet, roving life, divided into small bands that wandered incessantly in chase of the buffalo and the antelope. Their clothing was made from antelope skins, their diet was principally buffalo meat, and their homes were conical tents covered with buffalo hides. It was, therefore, only natural that the Indians devoted nearly all their energies to hunting the two animals so indispensable to their welfare. When the buffalo were scattered in small numbers over a plain, they stalked them singly and shot them with their bows and arrows; but at certain seasons, when the animals roamed the prairies in large herds, they organized large hunting parties to drive them into enclosures, or pounds, where they could destroy entire herds without danger. These organized buffalo hunts were really the outstanding activity in the lives of the Plains' Indians, who regulated them very strictly, and punished severely any one who disobeyed an order, frightened the animals even inadvertently, or in any way endangered the success of the hunt.

An early explorer, Henry, has vividly

described the buffalo hunting of the Assiniboine, who were considered more expert than the other two Plains' tribes in the construction of "pounds."

"The pounds are of different dimensions, according to the number of tents in one camp. The common size is from sixty to one hundred paces or yards in circumference, and about five feet in height. Trees are cut down, laid upon one another, and interwoven with branches and green twigs. . . . The entrance is about ten paces wide, and always fronts the plains. On each side of this entrance commences a thick range of fascines (pointed stakes), the two ranges spreading asunder as they extend, to the distance of one hundred yards, beyond which openings are left at intervals . . . and continue to spread apart to the right and left, until each range has been extended about three hundred yards from the pound. . . . Young men are usually sent out to collect and bring in the buffalo—a tedious task which requires great patience, for the herd must be started by slow degrees. This is done by setting fire to dung or grass. Three young men will bring in a herd from a great distance. When the wind is aft it is most favourable, as they can then direct the buffalo with great ease. Having come in sight of the ranges, they generally drive the herd faster, until it begins to enter the ranges, where a swift-footed person has been stationed with a buffalo robe over his head to imitate that animal.

47

. . . When he sees buffaloes approaching, he moves slowly toward the pound, until they appear to follow him; then he sets off at full speed, imitating a buffalo as well as he can, with the herd after him. The young men in the rear now . . . drive the herd on with all possible speed. . . . Every man, woman and child runs to the ranges that lead to the pound to prevent the buffalo from taking a wrong direction. . . . When the buffalo have been thus directed to the entrance of the pound the Indian who leads them rushes into it and out at the other side, either by jumping over the inclosure or creeping through an opening left for that purpose. The buffalo tumble in pell-mell at his heels, almost exhausted, but keep moving around the inclosure from east to west, and never in a direction against the sun. . . . Many buffaloes break their legs, and some their necks, in jumping into the pound, as the descent is generally six or eight feet, and stumps are left standing there. The buffalo being caught, the men assemble at the inclosure, armed with bows and arrows; every arrow has a particular mark of the owner, and they fly until the whole herd is killed."

The horse, spreading north from Mexico, reached the Canadian prairies early in the 18th century. Once introduced, it became an all-important factor in the lives of the Indians, and quickly spread from one tribe to another. It gave the Indians an unexpected mobility,

BLACKFOOT CROSSING THE ELBOW RIVER, ALBERTA

and vastly increased the range of their movements. The ease with which they could now run down whole herds of buffalo on horseback caused new tribes to encroach on their territory. It induced Indians from British Columbia to cross the Rocky Mountains each summer to share in the hunting, and Cree Indians to abandon the forested country in northern Saskatchewan and Manitoba and to make a fourth Plains' tribe permanently settled on the prairies.

Unhappily the horse also caused great rivalry between the tribes, and the once peaceful plains became a battling ground of natives who jostled on each other's hunting territories and fought at the slightest pretext. The organized methods they used in buffalo hunting now served them for military expeditions; new customs, new institutions, arose with amazing rapidity; and every tribe was put on a permanent war basis. The firearms that were introduced a few years later added to the reign of terror, and made the killing of the buffalo so easy that from the firing of the first musket the herds were doomed. The horse was not only an incentive to battle, but a medium of exchange, replacing the buffalo hides that now became so common as to be almost worthless. With horses the Indian bought his wife, and purchased long-coveted "medicine-bundles" that gave him power and prestige in his tribe; and "honourable" raids for the stealing of horses kept every camp in a constant state of alarm. Thus, in little more than a century, primitive tribes of hunters living a more or less isolated existence were changed into organized bands of daring warriors whose raids extended over thousands of miles, and whose hostility proved a formidable stumbling-block to the early colonization of the prairies by European settlers.

Prior to this reign of warfare the organization of the Plains' tribes was very loose and simple; but for warfare they needed a more compact government. Their political unit still remained the band, which was a group of families more or less closely related that hunted together and pitched their tents beside one another. Each band had its leader, who was chosen for certain outstanding qualities, principally for prowess in battle. During the summer most, if not all, of the wandering

bands joined together for several weeks and
set up their tents in a circle. The chief of one
band then became by common consent the
chief of the entire tribe and pitched his tent in
the middle; but his authority was so limited
that he had to refer all important matters to a
council, consisting of all the other band chiefs
and a few of the leading warriors.

This summer gathering offered one of the
most picturesque scenes. The tents, or tipis,
in which the Indians lived were conical frame-
works of poles covered with from twelve to
twenty buffalo hides. Two ears or lugs at
the top served as chimneys; the door was a
slit in the wall protected with a small flap.
Many tents were decorated with vividly-
painted designs, some representing war-deeds,
others mystic scenes that the owners of the
tents had dreamed in their youth, when they
fasted in solitude and prayed for blessings
from the spirit world. At outposts near the
tribal camp-circle were the picketed horses,
where gaily mounted young men paraded up
and down to guard against sudden raids.
Dignified warriors strolled from tent to tent
to discuss matters of special import, and to

TYPICAL TIPIS OF THE PLAINS
Formerly of buffalo-hide, now of cloth.

Photo by *Harlan I. Smith.*

maintain order in the camp. The women, clad in painted robes, scraped skins, sewed moccasins, and prepared the family meals over small outdoor fires, using, instead of the clay pots or bark vessels of the Eastern Indians, bags of skin, which they filled with meat and water and heated with red-hot stones. When the chief gave orders to move away, the women unpitched the tents, packed up the household possessions, and followed in the tracks of the warriors, who rode in front and on each flank to guard the train from attack.

Besides its bands each tribe of Plains' Indians evolved societies or fraternities whose members could belong to any band, and whose leaders had seats in the tribal council. These societies temporarily dissolved when the bands wandered apart from one another, but received very important functions when they united. Their members then policed the tribal camp, kept guard against enemies, and carried out special duties in connection with the buffalo hunt. Each of the societies held an annual dance, and during the two or three days that the dance lasted, exercised more authority in the camp than the tribal chief and his council.

54

Indians of the Plains

It was during the summer gathering of the bands that the Plains' Indians held their most striking festival, the Sun-Dance, which was not an annual performance, but occurred only at intervals of two or three years. The actual rites varied with the different tribes, but everywhere the main purpose of the festival was to offer up thanks to the Great Spirit. Though the Indians worshipped many of the powers of nature, they regarded even the greatest of them, the sun and the thunder, merely as separate instruments of the one Great Spirit who ruled over all things. At their Sun-Dance festival they erected in the centre of their camp a sacred pole that they had cut in the woods and gleefully dragged to the site like a captive enemy. To this pole they fastened various offerings for the Great Spirit, pieces of skin or cloth, ornaments and other objects that, however small, yet represented some sacrifice on the part of the giver. Then they danced around it, recited valorous war deeds, thanked the Great Spirit for past favours, and prayed for guidance and blessings during the coming months. In some tribes two or three young braves allowed their chests to be pierced with skewers that were attached to the sacred pole by stout thongs, and they tugged with all their strength against the thongs until they broke free, or friends took pity on their fainting condition and released them. This self-inflicted torture, they hoped, would arouse the compassion of the Great Spirit and gain them special favours and help. The essential rites lasted four days, but since the whole tribe united only once a year, the Indians extended the festival in order to perform other religious ceremonies, to sing and dance, and to indulge in games and banqueting. One tribe had a ceremonial buffalo-hunt immediately before the festival. In other tribes individuals carried out some of the rites required for the purchase of sacred "medicine-bundles." For most of the people, however, it was a time of keen enjoyment, with more stress laid on conviviality than on the religious features of the festival.

CHAPTER V

TRIBES OF THE PACIFIC COAST

THE natives on the Pacific coast of
Canada differed in almost every respect
from the other Indians of the Dominion. In
appearance they distinctly resembled the
Mongolian race, partly, perhaps, owing to
recent intermarriage with Chinese immigrants,
but mainly because they were descended from
Asiatic peoples who carried in their veins an
extra heavy strain of Mongolian blood. Just
as they differed in appearance from the tribes
to the east, so they differed in their manners
and customs, their food, their clothing, their
houses, and their arts and crafts.

For food they depended almost entirely on
fish and sea-mammals. Agriculture was altogether unknown, and the land animals so
necessary to the Eastern Indians were too
scarce to be of much importance. While sea-
mammals and shell-fish were highly valued,
the natives lived principally on fish. Each
year several species of salmon migrated up
the rivers, sometimes in such numbers that
they piled in the canyons like logs in a jam.

APPROXIMATE DISTRIBUTION OF PACIFIC COAST TRIBES IN 1725 A.D.

The Indians speared them in hundreds from the banks, or, more often, checked their progress with elaborate log weirs and caught them in traps and baskets. Besides salmon, they caught herring and halibut in the bays and estuaries, using for halibut a bone hook and a line of twisted cedar-bark. They caught also the tiny oolakan, a fish, still highly prized for its oil, which shoals in vast numbers, early in the spring, at the mouths of certain rivers. All along the coast they captured seals, sea-lions and sea-otters, the beauty of the sea-otter skins being the lure that attracted the earliest fur-traders to their shores. The Nootka Indians hunted even the whales that frequented the west coast of Vancouver Island, but their pursuit in dug-out canoes, with only hand-harpoons for weapons and paddles for speed, required amazing courage and skill.

The division of labour threw the fishing and hunting entirely on the men, but the women gathered shellfish of many species from the seashore, and, as amongst other tribes, great quantities of berries and edible roots which they dried and stored for the winter.

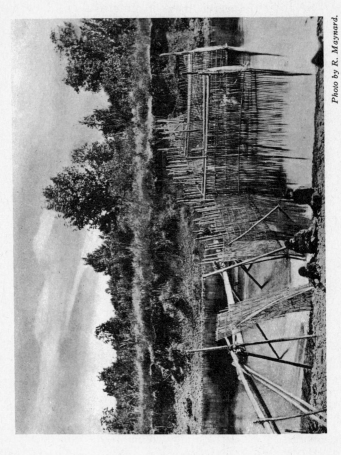

Photo by R. Maynard.

A SALMON-WEIR ON THE COWICHAN RIVER, B.C.

Tribes of the Pacific Coast

Nowhere in Canada, not even among the Iroquois whose "long-houses" were stoutly made and semi-permanent abodes, did the natives build dwellings as imposing as those on the Pacific coast. The inhabitants of this region, though hunters and fishermen ignorant of agriculture, were, nevertheless, a more or less sedentary people. The wealth of the sea enabled them at any season of the year to gather enough food for their wants within a radius of a few miles; thus they remained in the same villages year after year for many generations. They had a genius, too, for carpentry, and in the giant cedar trees that flourished all along their coast possessed a straight-grained timber easily split with bone wedges and hammers of stone. Their houses were of two types, both constructed of cedar logs and planks. In the Fraser Delta and along the southern shores of Vancouver Island they erected huge sheds, often several hundred feet long, with gently sloping roofs. Inside they left a passage-way down the middle and divided the rest of the space into "stalls," much in the way that we divide our cattle-barns; and they allotted to each family one of the small open stalls. The second type of house, used farther north, was square or oblong in shape, and had a gabled roof with enormous cedar logs forming the rafters. In a chief's house the corner posts, and the pillars that held up the rafters, were often carved with human or animal figures; and the centre post in front was a totem-pole so large that the doorway was merely the yawning mouth of one of its carved figures, a bear, perhaps, or a whale. Weirdly painted, too, were the boards, three to five feet broad, that formed the pediment underneath the gable. When we realize that in the old days the Indians had only the crudest of tools, no machinery whatsoever, and did not even know the principle of the wheel or pulley, we can appreciate how much labour it must have involved to fell the trees, dress the lumber with stone-bladed adzes, raise the huge beams into place, and adjust the heavy boards, without a single nail to hold the enormous structure together.

The average West Coast family was not blessed with many household goods, though the chiefs naturally possessed more than their humbler retainers. The most conspicuous

Photo by G. M. Dawson.

SKEDANS

A Haida Indian village on the Queen Charlotte Islands.

pieces of "furniture," of which every chief's family owned several, were cleverly constructed cedar chests, each made from one plank bent into a quadrangle and sewed or dowelled at the fourth corner, with a bottom board fitted in by mortising, and a detachable lid. The Indians expended much labour in painting and carving these chests, which they used for every conceivable purpose. They stored in them not only their food—fish, meat, berries, roots and oil—but also their woven bark clothes, and the precious regalia that they wore at feasts and dances. Besides the chests there were cedar-bark mats of various sizes that were used for curtains, floor-rugs and bedding. Baskets made of roots, weapons for hunting and fishing, tools for woodwork, and a varied assortment of carved bowls, spoons and ladles made of wood or horn completed the household furnishings.

Owing to the mildness of their climate, the Coast Indians might have dispensed with clothing altogether during the greater part of the year. As it was, most of them made their costumes entirely of woven cedar-bark, and utilized animal skins only for rich ceremonial

64

robes. Both men and women wore oblong
cedar-bark cloaks fastened over one shoulder
and under the other. In rainy or chilly
weather they added a rain-cape made of the
same material, and a conical or dome-shaped
hat of woven spruce roots. An apron fastened
under the cloak took the place of trousers or
breech-cloth; and though both sexes sometimes
wore moccasins, usually they preferred to
leave their feet bare. All the tribes delighted
in ornaments of various kinds, bracelets,
anklets, and peculiar, oval-shaped objects
inserted into the under-lip that are commonly
known as labrets. Here and there along the
coast individuals decorated their faces and
bodies with tattooing, but this ornamentation
was not common outside the Queen Charlotte
Islands.

The art of the West Coast Indians has
attracted more notice than the art of other
Canadian tribes on account of its bizarre and
exotic character. Even before they were
visited by white men they had developed extra-
ordinary skill in wood-carving and wood-
painting. The sudden advent of iron tools,
far superior to their old stone ones, gave to

their art an amazing impetus, and the totem-poles, carved house-pillars and carved boxes that had once been the exclusive property of chiefs depreciated in value until they came within the reach of the common people. Most of the carvings and paintings represented animals, fish, birds, or supernatural beings that the Indians saw, or imagined they saw, around them; but these subjects were generally treated in such a strange, conventional manner that Europeans often fail to understand or appreciate them. The same striking animal designs were carried out in wool-weaving by the Tsimshian and Tlinkit Indians, whose "Chilkat" blankets of mountain-goat wool mixed with shredded cedar-bark showed rare artistry combined with unusually fine weaving. Much less attractive were the blankets made by the Salish Indians of the Fraser River, who combined dog's hair with their wool, and confined their decorative patterns to geometric figures. The Salish, and the Nootka Indians of Vancouver Island, were proficient also in the making of baskets from spruce and other roots, an industry that still thrives under modern conditions, whereas the "Chilkat

66

blanket" is now practically a thing of the past, preserved only in museums.

Among the many ceremonies, social and religious, peculiar to the Pacific Coast Indians, the potlatch, now for many years forbidden by the Canadian Government, held the foremost place. In former years the giving of pot-latches was the royal road, in fact the only road, to power and prestige; they marked every stage in the career of a high-born Indian, from the ceremony in which he first received a name to his death and burial. Essentially they were lavish feasts accompanied by a distribution of presents for the purpose of enhancing the prestige of the host. However, so intricate and varied were the ceremonies connected with them, that the mere description of their details would fill many volumes. Potlatches were held on all possible occasions. The highest ambition of every man was to celebrate one more extravagantly than his fellows, and chiefs vied in liberality with one another merely to add personal glory and prestige to their names. The gifts—which included the Indians' most prized possessions, robes, skins, boxes, blankets, and immense

TSIMSHIAN INDIAN

Wearing a wooden head-dress inlaid with abalone shell and a woven "Chilkat" blanket of goat's wool and cedar bark.

quantities of food—were often not true gifts at all. In reality they became debts, forced on distinguished guests and repayable with interest at later potlatches, for it was the custom always to give a larger gift than you had received. In such cases the host not only gained honor for being a generous giver, but was assured of receiving later on much more than he had expended on his feast.

Of all the Indian systems of government, that of the Pacific Coast tribes was the most intricate and spectacular. Society was built on a definite caste basis, the natives being divided into three grades, nobles, common people and slaves, that did not often intermarry. The nobles claimed possession of all the land and of all the places for fishing and hunting. Each of their families owned many slaves to do the manual work, and kept as retainers a large body of common people who clung to them for protection. The slaves were prisoners of war or their offspring, who enjoyed no rights of any kind, but were sold from tribe to tribe like furniture.

The smallest political unit was the village. The largest was also the village, or more often a number of villages close together whose inhabitants spoke the same dialect, had the same mode of life, intermarried and relied on each other for protection. Every village had one or more leaders, the nobles who had the largest followings. When we speak of a tribe on the Pacific Coast we do not mean a political unit, but all the villages over a wide area whose inhabitants spoke the same language, even though they recognized no common leadership, and indeed often made war on one another.

Several families of nobles, again, though dwelling in different villages, constituted a clan; and each clan had its emblem or coat-of-arms which its nobles carved on their totem-poles, painted on the fronts of their houses, and carved or painted on their boxes. The emblem was usually a supernatural animal, such as a monstrous bear, that had supposedly made itself known to the mythical founder of the clan. In the north of British Columbia two tribes merged their clans into two divisions that they named Ravens and Eagles, or, in some districts, Ravens and Wolves. All men and women who fell into the Raven (or

TLINKIT MEDICINE-MAN AND HIS INCANTATIONS

the Eagle) division considered themselves closely related; they could not intermarry, could not even bury their own dead; and, if they belonged to different villages or tribes that were at war, they tried to avoid each other in battle. But the Indians in the south of British Columbia rejected this larger grouping, and attached very little importance even to their clans.

This intricate political system differed in one great respect from the organization of the Iroquois tribes, the only other with which it might be compared. The Iroquois were deeply interested in the theory and practice of government, and possessed a spirit of real imperialism. The Pacific Coast peoples had little political consciousness. Their main interest lay not in government but in social activities, in ceremonies and potlatches, in pomp and display, and in the acquisition of wealth to advance themselves and their families one more rung upon the social ladder.

Their religious beliefs did not differ greatly from those of other Indians. They thought that supernatural beings surrounded them on every side, in the woods, in the trees, and

72

especially in the waters. While they recognized vaguely one supreme sky-god, to whom they occasionally prayed, they devoted most of their prayers and sacrifices to the ocean deities, on whose good will they relied for their daily supply of salmon and other sea-foods. Their ideas of the after-life were very indefinite. Man's ghost, they thought, remained on earth after death, while his soul went to another country, possibly to the sky. However, as the sky-land was not necessarily a better or happier place than this earth, they looked forward to the change with little joy. Each tribe on the coast had its own manner of disposing of the dead. Cremation, common amongst the northern tribes, became rare farther south, where the Indians laid out their dead in mortuary houses, or in coffins placed in trees or on carved posts. In a few places they buried their dead in the ground, or in natural caves along the coast.

Chapter VI

PLATEAU TRIBES OF BRITISH COLUMBIA

THE interior plateau of British Columbia, separated off from the coast by the line of the Cascade Range, and from the Great Plains by the Rocky Mountains, formed a melting pot for offshoots of various tribes of Indians who came there, voluntarily or by force, from the north, the south and the east. Classified roughly as "Plateau Tribes" they were a decidedly motley group, having different origins, different languages, and even cultures that failed to become alike owing to the difficulties of communication in this rugged section.

The largest sub-group, the Interior Salish, inhabited the basin of the Fraser River, and was made up of five tribes, Lillooet, Thompson, Okanagan, Lake and Shuswap, who originally entered Canada from the south. The Coast Salish Indians, and the Bella Coola, were offshoots of this group who had settled on the coast, where they had allowed their

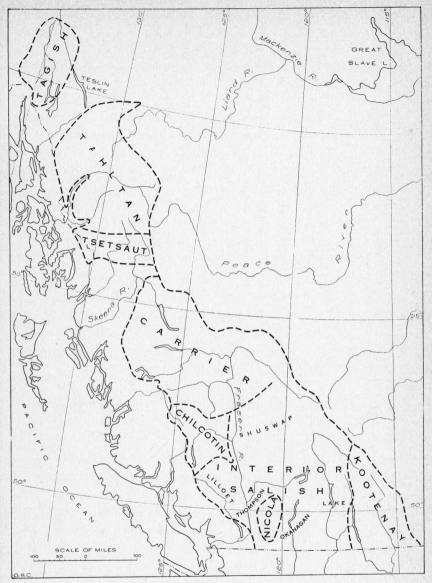

APPROXIMATE DISTRIBUTION OF PLATEAU TRIBES IN 1725 A.D.

earlier culture to be swamped by the intricate coast system. In the basin of the Kootenay River dwelt the Kootenay, a definitely Plains' people who had been driven over the Rockies by the Blackfoot Indians early in the 18th century, but who tenaciously held to their Plains' characteristics. Of the five tribes that occupied the northern part of the plateau the largest were the Carrier, who lived along the line of the present transcontinental railway between Prince George and Hazelton, and the Tahltan, who occupied the basin of the Stikine River. These northern tribes all spoke dialects of a single language, Athabaskan, but in manners and customs they were very unlike, and, having no common interests they tended to take on the colour of the coastal Indians, whose richer life exerted an irresistible attraction for them, and whose settlements were comparatively accessible down the westward-flowing rivers.

In certain customs, however, the Plateau tribes withstood the influence of the coast. Their dress, owing to the severer climate, remained similar to that of the Indians east of the Rockies; tunics, leggings, moccasins

76

and robes for colder weather, formed the costume for men, women and children alike.
Though their dwellings were not the same in
every district, they, too, were free from
western influence. The Interior Salish Indians
and some of their neighbours in the south
built for winter a unique semi-underground
log house, about forty feet in diameter, with
an entrance through the roof. In summer,
when these dwellings became damp and
untenable, they moved into oblong or conical
lodges covered with rush mats or brush. The
Kootenay tribe, during the entire year, preferred the conical Plains' tipi, covered with
painted buffalo hides wherever available, with
rush mats as a secondary choice. Farther
north the tribes lived in gabled rectangular
huts of logs or poles, built above ground, and
covered with layers of spruce bark.

The rivers that interlace the whole of the
plateau country teemed with salmon, and the
lakes contained abundant carp and other fish
that the Indians caught under the ice in
winter. The woodland sections of the country
abounded in game—caribou, moose, bear, porcupine, beaver and smaller species. So fish

CARRIER INDIAN WOMAN DRESSING A MOOSEHIDE WITH
A STONE-BLADED SCRAPER

and game in fairly equal measure were the staple food of all the tribes. In summer the salmon that migrated up the rivers from the sea supplied most of their needs; during the same season, the wild berries and roots that grow profusely in the interior were gathered by the women and dried in the sun to preserve for times of less abundance. In winter most of the tribes devoted their whole time to hunting and trapping, and during those months their principal food was meat, eked out with the few fish which they caught through the ice. The Kootenay of the Upper Columbia River, and a few Shuswap on the South Thompson River (where the salmon were of inferior quality owing to their long journey from the sea), relied very little upon fish, but crossed the Rockies each summer to roam the prairies in search of buffalo, whose flesh they ate, and whose skins they used for their conical tipis.

The Plateau tribes had various ways of cooking, but generally roasted their meat and fish suspended over a fire on sticks. A few natives living nearest the sea adopted the coast practice of boiling their food in water-tight wooden boxes; and all the tribes knew the method of boiling in water-proof kettles of bark or woven spruce roots.

Travelling in this rugged region offered many difficulties, which the Indians only partly overcame. The Okanagan tribe, and its neighbour, the Kootenay, used peculiar canoes that were pointed under water at each end, a shape adopted by no other Indians in America, although found on the Amur River in northeastern Siberia. But both the Okanagan canoes and those of the other Plateau tribes were poorly made from pine- or spruce-bark, and utterly unsuited for navigating the swift rivers full of rapids and canyons. For winter travel the natives had neither sled nor toboggan, and the few snowshoes that were made in the southern districts were far inferior to those of the Eastern Indians. Consequently, winter and summer alike, the natives were forced to travel mainly on foot.

The political life of those tribes that were least affected by coastal and other influences resembled the simple organization of the hunting tribes of Eastern Canada. It was founded on the family and the band, which was a group

A KOOTENAY CHIEF

A typical Indian of the plains, although his home lies west of the Rocky
Mountains.

of families related by blood or marriage. Each band had its leader whose office usually descended to his son; but the real authority lay with an informal council of the older men and the most prominent hunters. Each band had also its own hunting and fishing territory, held in common by all its families, who generally wandered and hunted together. This simple structure of society became submerged, however, wherever there was close contact with natives from the coast, for then the inland people adopted the clan system, the potlatch, masked dances, and some of the secret medicine rites. Two or three tribes even borrowed the division into castes, and separated their members into nobles, commoners and slaves.

In their religious life all the Plateau tribes clung to their original beliefs, over which any ideas they accepted from the coast settled as a thin veneer. The ocean deities to whom the coast natives sacrificed did not concern them. The Kootenay Indians offered most of their prayers and sacrifices to the Sun-God, believing, as perhaps did all the Plains' tribes originally, that it was the Sun-God who reigned supreme. They believed also, that the souls of their dead would one day come to life near Lake Pend-Oreille, and, to hasten the day of return, held a religious ceremony on the shores of that lake at irregular intervals. Other tribes, too, had singular beliefs concerning the life after death. The Tahltan thought that the soul of a much-loved tribesman could find reincarnation a year or two after death, if one of his kinswomen performed a sacred rite to bring about the rebirth in her next child. The Interior Salish placed their faith in a mythical keeper of souls, the "Chief of the Dead," and every year or two held a series of feasts at which they bathed, fasted and prayed that he would guard them against future ills. Festivals, however, whether religious or social, were much less common than on the coast, for food was never plentiful, and hunting kept the members of the tribes more scattered. Medicine-men, as among all Indians, used their power for both good and evil, and over these Plateau people exerted considerable influence. The chief desire, not only of the medicine-men, but of every native, was to obtain for himself guardian spirits; and boys (rarely also girls) sometimes fasted and prayed in solitude for as long as two or three years, in order to obtain from these spirits the necessary revelations.

Death customs varied from one tribe to another. In the south most of the Indians buried their dead in the ground or under piles of rocks; in the north they usually cremated the bodies and scattered the ashes to the winds. The Carrier Indians owe their name to the gruesome custom of forcing every widow to carry her dead husband's ashes on her back, and to become a bond-slave to his relatives, until her period of mourning ended.

The arts of painting, wood-carving and wool-weaving, as we have seen them on the coast, did not exist amongst these less progressive tribes of the Plateau. Any painting or carving they may have given to their dwellings or mortuary houses was borrowed wholly from their more artistic neighbours; and many of their personal ornaments were derived in trade from the same source. But another type of art, the weaving of baskets, reached a very high development amongst the Indians of the Fraser and Thompson River valleys. Tribes

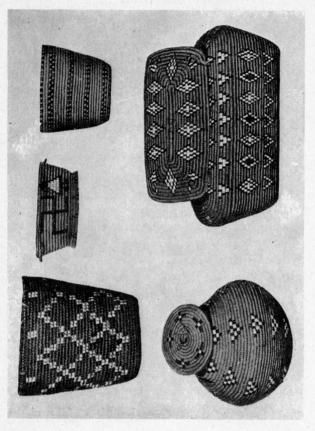

Photo by National Museum of Canada.

COILED BASKETS OF THE THOMPSON RIVER INDIANS

to the northward made only rough vessels of bark or plaited spruce roots, but these Interior Salish natives wove beautiful coiled baskets, decorated with animal, bird and geometric designs, by an overlay process known as imbrication. In earlier days, though their workmanship was just as fine, they knew but a limited number of shapes; but since their baskets have found a ready sale amongst the white people they have varied the shapes to suit the larger market, and their products are now known to American and European collectors as the finest and most artistic in the Dominion.

CHAPTER VII

TRIBES OF THE MACKENZIE AND YUKON BASINS

SCATTERED tribes living in the basins of the Mackenzie and Yukon Rivers comprise the sixth geographic group of Indians in the Dominion. Each tribe differed from its neighbours in varying degrees, but they all spoke dialects of a single language, Athabaskan, the only tongue in Canada that has been found to preserve definite traces of Asiatic origin. Like many languages of Eastern Asia, it has a tonal system that gives it a slightly sing-song character, and certain words show a noticeable relationship to earliest Chinese.

With neighbours not more than a few hundred miles away having a civilization as rich and bizarre as that of the West Coast tribes, one marvels at the primitiveness of these northern people. They resembled far more the homely wandering tribes of the eastern woodlands, but lacked the cheerfulness of the eastern people, and were even less progres-

87

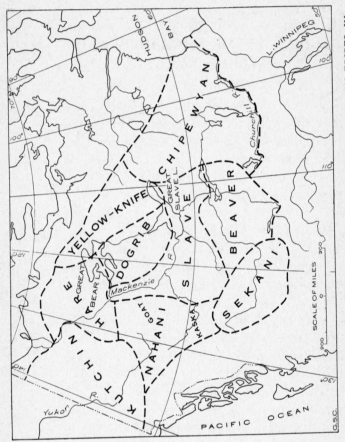

APPROXIMATE DISTRIBUTION OF MACKENZIE RIVER AND YUKON TRIBES IN
1725 A.D.

sive. No doubt their backwardness was partly due to the country they inhabited. Their forests were far less rich in game than the woods of Ontario, Quebec or the Maritimes; the climate was harsher, the changes of season more severe. Moreover, the natives themselves did not have the same contact as the Algonkians with peoples more advanced than themselves. Where they did encounter tribes higher in the scale of culture, they quickly assimilated foreign traits, and their lives took on a more picturesque aspect.

The Kutchin tribe, which occupied the basin of the Yukon, traded with both Eskimo and natives from the Pacific coast, and their social life and material culture, enriched by borrowings from these neighbours, are far more attractive than those of their isolated kinsmen in the basin of the Mackenzie. In historic times, also, two of the more southern tribes, the Chipewyan and the Beaver, adopted the customs and manners of the warring Cree from the east, who penetrated farther and farther into their country after the introduction of firearms. But no stimulus from outside reached the majority of the Mackenzie

Indians, who lived in an isolation more or less complete.

All these northern people were primarily hunters and forest dwellers. Two or three tribes only, who lived east of the Mackenzie River, deserted the woods in summer to pursue herds of caribou on the open barren-ground; yet they, too, in winter returned to the woodland. Everywhere in the forests they found caribou, beaver and hare; and, in the more southern districts, bear, moose and buffalo. When hunting caribou they built fences of brush in which they left gaps for the placing of snares; on the barren-grounds, where there was no brush or timber, they drove the animals into the water and speared them from canoes. Their weapons were bows and arrows, clubs fashioned from bone or antler, and spears pointed with stone, bone, or in some districts copper. They relied less on their weapons, however, than on snares of caribou raw-hide, set in many different ways, with which they caught animals of every kind from the tiny marmot to the ungainly moose.

Though hunting was their chief occupation, most of the tribes resorted to the rivers and

Photo by D. Jenness.

A SEKANI HUT OF POLES AND SPRUCE BARK

lakes during the summer when caribou and other game were difficult to find. There they fished with nets of twisted willow-bark or raw-hide, sometimes also with hand lines, and, in the rivers of the Yukon, weirs and traps.

Their homes were as primitive as their lives. Nearly all the tribes had conical lodges of poles, carelessly covered with bark or caribou skin, which served either for summer or winter. During the summer they sometimes used mere shelters or lean-tos of brush, that gave little protection against wind and rain. Certain tribes living along the Mackenzie built in winter low, oblong cabins of poles, the top roofed with spruce boughs and the walls chinked with sods of moss. No less meagre and cheerless was the inside of their dwellings. Brush covered the floor, and a few skins thrown down in the back of the lodge provided beds and bedding. Furniture hardly existed. The natives' only possessions were bows and arrows, spears, axes, knives, tools for scraping skins, bags of solid skin or netted thong for carrying their belongings, and the women's cooking vessels of bark or tightly-woven spruce roots. For transport they had toboggans for winter, and poorly made canoes of spruce-bark or (rarely) birch-bark for summer; but neither of these equalled in their manufacture the toboggans or canoes of the east.

Clothing was usually of caribou skin, and closely resembled that of the Eastern and Plains' Indians. The men wore a sleeveless shirt, sometimes laced together between the legs, leggings that reached to the thighs, and moccasins with insoles of fur; the women wore a longer shirt and leggings that came only to the knees. A robe, cap and mittens provided extra warmth for winter. A few of the tribes joined moccasins and leggings together, and some joined shirt and cap to form a hood. In districts where moose and caribou were scarce the women and children often dressed in garments of woven hare-skin. The Kutchin, who had contact with the Eskimo, partly adopted their style of dress. They wore the long-tailed Eskimo shirt, which the women sometimes enlarged at the back to carry their babies; and their leggings, joined to the moccasins, were so full that they resembled Eskimo long-boots. All the tribes decorated their costumes with fringes, and many added embroidery of porcupine quill or moose hair. They were fond of ornaments of a simple character, and wore bracelets and armlets of bone or horn, or sometimes of leather embroidered with porcupine quills. A necklet, especially prized by the men in some localities, was made from grizzly bear claws, or from polished tips of caribou antler. The Kutchin, whose dress was more attractive than that of the other tribes, daubed their faces with red and black paint, put bright feathers in their hair, and hung elaborate pendants of dentalia shell from their costumes, their necks, and even from their noses and ears.

None of these tribes had any permanent villages, and their political organization was exceedingly simple. Only the Nahani Indians of the Upper Liard River, and the Kutchin, developed a feeble clan system, borrowed with other foreign elements from the West Coast Indians with whom they had direct or indirect trade. Amongst the other tribes the family was the unit, and groups of related families formed bands whose leaders had little or no authority, and held their positions by person-

A KUTCHIN CHIEF WITH ORNAMENTS OF DENTALIUM SHELLS

(Reproduced from Sir J. Richardson, *Arctic Searching Expedition, A Journal of a Boat Voyage through Rupert's Land and the Arctic Sea*, Vol. I, Pl. VII, London, 1851).

ality alone. Few feasts or ceremonies bright-
ened the dull monotony of their lives; but the
natives threw themselves whole-heartedly into
gambling games of various kinds. Each band
had its own hunting territory, but the country
was so vast and so sparsely populated that
boundaries were vaguely defined, and trespass-
ing was neither serious nor common. The
tribe was not really a political unit, but merely
a group of bands speaking the same dialect
and living on friendly terms. There were no
keepers of law and order; when disputes arose,
an informal council of hunters settled them by
ordering compensation or by pacifying the
offended in other ways. Marriage was regulated according to the degree of relationship,
and as usual, men were allowed more than
one wife. Often, in fact, they staged wrestling bouts in which the wives of the weaker
men went to the victors. In most of the tribes
women had a harder lot than anywhere else
in the Dominion. Girl babies that were a
burden to their mothers were often killed at
birth; and the old and infirm were regularly
abandoned to die of starvation and exposure.
To us, who extend the same care and protec-

tion to our aged as we do to children, this seems unspeakably cruel, but it was almost inevitable among a people who were forced to move on, without vehicles, day after day, in order to obtain their food and clothing. Even so, periods of starvation were frequent; and when food was scarce it was always the weaker members of the band, rather than the hunters, who had to go hungry.

The thought of death, however, did not fill the Indians with horror or apprehension. They accepted it philosophically as the natural end of life, and vaguely conceived that the souls of the good might travel on to a beautiful land, abounding in game, to which the wicked souls could not attain. When sickness overtook them they often confessed their sins, but this was rather to delay the approach of death than to ensure the entrance of their souls into a happy hereafter. Unlike other tribes they had no important deities to whom they offered prayers and sacrifices, though they made petty offerings at times to propitiate local spirits thought to dwell in the woods and waters. Their chief belief was in the existence of guardian spirits. Every young man fasted for several days alone in the forest, and returned home only after ⋅he had acquired, through a dream, the guardianship of an animal or supernatural being. This remained his guardian throughout life, but was appealed to only in times of stress or danger. Men who, in later life, acquired other dream guardians, and claimed direct contact with the supernatural world, became medicine-men, and were held in great awe by the natives as witch-doctors who could both cause and cure disease.

The northern Indians lacked the knowledge of herbal remedies possessed by the Eastern Woodlands' tribes, but used the same type of shaking lodge in performing their rites. When the power of the medicine-man failed and death occurred, the natives gave themselves over to an elaborate display of grief. They destroyed all their property, and gashed their bodies; the women cut off their hair or even their fingers, and went into mourning for a year. The tribes disposed of their dead in different ways. Some covered the body with leaves or brush inside a small hut containing the property of the deceased; others placed

Photo by R. Bell.

A CHIPEWYAN CAMP NEAR CHURCHILL, HUDSON BAY

the body on scaffolds or in trees. One tribe burned its dead, either immediately or a year after death, and scattered the ashes to the four winds; and others merely left the bodies where they lay, to be devoured by the animals and birds of the forest.

Each group of tribes throughout the Dominion has shown certain outstanding characteristics that distinguish it from its neighbours. The ingenious use of birch-bark for canoes, dwellings and household utensils, we associate with the wandering tribes of the Eastern Woodlands. Agriculture, and the semi-sedentary life that its practice involved, moulded the lives of the Iroquoian tribes, those forceful, politically-minded nations who had within them the ambitious spirit of empire-builders. On the plains lived nomadic tribes of daring buffalo-hunters. On the Pacific Coast, the home of the salmon and the cedar, slave-owning peoples developed art and drama to heights seldom reached in savage communities, and spread the influence of their culture eastward to colour the lives of the Plateau tribes. But our survey of the tribes in the Mackenzie and Yukon basins leaves us without any tangible picture. They were lacking in outstanding features, were devoid of those definite traits that reveal a distinct individuality. They lived precarious lives in harsh surroundings, and lacked the stamina and courage to rise above their environment and poverty. One day followed another in the dull monotony of pitching and breaking camp, always in search of game; and there were few ceremonies or dances to brighten their leisure hours. Perhaps they were the weaklings of their stock, as some writers believe, left behind in the north when their more enterprising kinsmen pushed southwest and south, to become the Sarcee of the plains, the allies of the Blackfoot, and the Carrier and other tribes in the interior of British Columbia.

Chapter VIII

THE ESKIMO

A S late as 1902 there were tribes of
Eskimo living on the Arctic shores of
Canada who had not come into contact with
white men since the middle of the 19th century, who were still living in an age of stone,
and who were almost totally ignorant of the
world outside their own limited spaces of ice
and snow. They realized vaguely that there
were other Eskimo dwelling far to the east,
and perhaps also far to the west. They knew
that to the south of them dwelt Indians,
wicked, hostile people whom they greatly
feared, and from whom they carefully kept
aloof; but only one or two of the oldest inhabitants had ever seen a white man, and their
feeble memories recalled them as strange,
incomprehensible people, who were possibly
not human beings at all.

These little known Eskimo, who lived from
Coronation Gulf to the Magnetic Pole, were
but one group of the people who inhabited the
Arctic coastline, at intervals, all the way from

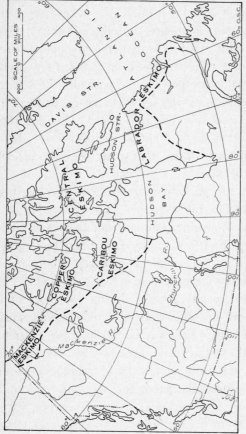

APPROXIMATE DISTRIBUTION OF THE ESKIMO IN 1525 A.D.

the Alaskan boundary to the southern edge of the Labrador Peninsula. All spoke dialects of a common language, and though each group had, with time and isolation, developed slightly different manners and customs, they were originally one people, and probably the last of the American aborigines to reach this continent from the Siberian shore. So different were they from Indians in appearance, dress and manner of life, that many scientists believe they belonged to a distinct race.

To the early explorers their lives seemed pitiable in the extreme. Their home was a dreary coastline, low and undulating in some places, high and rocky in others, but everywhere barren of all trees, except many miles inland up the valleys of one or two rivers. The ground, partly covered during the short summer season with grass and mosses and small flowering plants, was buried in snow for nine months of the year, and the sea was then frozen solid like the land. Except in Labrador, the sun disappeared altogether for two months in midwinter, and darkness prevailed except for a few hours of twilight at midday, and whatever light the moon afforded. In midsummer, on the other hand, the land was flooded with light, for the sun circled round the Arctic sky for a period corresponding to the period of darkness in winter. Any cultivation of the soil under such conditions was out of the question, and the only possible source of food lay in the game that the country could furnish. But the game, too, was limited, consisting principally of caribou on the land, and fish and seals in the water; on these the Eskimo had to depend for their existence.

They spent the winter months in spearing seals, while from May to November they hunted the caribou in the valleys and hills, and captured salmon and trout in the lakes and streams. A few small bands of inland Eskimo, dwelling on the barren grounds between Hudson Bay and Great Slave Lake, lived almost entirely on caribou, and seldom, if ever, visited the coast to hunt sea mammals. But these bands frequently suffered from famine, for when the caribou retreated to the woods toward midwinter, they had to fall back on the rare musk-oxen, and upon such fish as they could catch through the ice in the streams and lakes.

A LABRADOR ESKIMO HUNTER IN HIS KAYAK

Photo by F. Johansen

The Eskimo

For weapons the Eskimo used bows and arrows; spears and harpoons with tips of flint, ivory or bone, or of copper picked up on the surface of the ground and pounded into shape with stones; and knives, fish-hooks and other implements which they made of the same materials. There were two kinds of harpoons, one for spearing seals in the open sea during the spring and summer, the other for spearing them in winter when the sea was frozen over. At that season the animals maintained in the ice several breathing holes to which they periodically rose for air. Only the trained eye of an Eskimo, or the keen scent of his dog, could detect the tiny hole concealed beneath a foot or more of snow. Even when the hole had been discovered, there was no certainty that the seal would visit it for several hours. But the Eskimo never lost his game from lack of patience, and the hardships of a motionless watch, often for many hours at a time, exposed to all the rigours of an Arctic winter, counted as nothing if at last his harpoon struck true and he could drag home a fresh seal to his expectant family. In spring, when the seals came out of their holes to bask in the sun on the surface of the ice, the natives stalked them as they did the caribou and harpooned them from a distance. At the same season they harpooned them also from the edge of the ice-sheet, when lanes of water broke up its surface; and in summer they hunted them in the open sea in their skin-covered kayaks.

This seal-skin kayak was one of the cleverest inventions ever made by a primitive people. The Indians invented the birch-bark canoe; but for ingenuity of construction it could not compare with the Eskimo's one-man hunting boat, shaped like a racing-shell, and completely decked with skin, except for a round manhole a little back from the centre. Quite different was their *umiak* or travelling boat, which also had a covering of skin, but resembled in shape a European whale-boat. For travelling over the hard, snow-covered surface of the land and sea, every Eskimo family used the wooden sled, shod originally with bone or ivory, and drawn by a team of well-trained dogs; a more suitable vehicle even European explorers have not evolved for winter journeys in the Arctic.

In many other ways the Eskimo showed
their ingenuity. There were no trees in their
country to provide timber or bark, no bricks
or mortar to construct a house. In summer
they lived in tents of seal or caribou skin that
they carried on their backs from one place to
another; but for the winter they needed more
substantial dwellings to keep out the bitter
cold. In the Mackenzie River delta, where
driftwood brought down by the river piled up
on the beaches, they constructed semi-subter-
ranean houses of logs, which they covered with
moss and turf. Elsewhere driftwood was not
available, and they built dome-shaped snow-
huts of one or more connected rooms, whose
sole entrance was a small, round opening at
the bottom closed at night with a snow block.
The interior was remarkably warm and comfortable. Opposite the doorway was a low
platform covered with caribou skins, where
the inmates slept at night and worked during
the day. To the left, thrown upon the floor,
lay the hunter's catch, the carcase of a seal,
perhaps, or huge lumps of walrus meat. On
the right, supported by sticks, a heavy stone
lamp carved out of soapstone cast a soft glow

over the opaque walls, and at the same time cooked the evening meal of seal-meat in a soapstone pot suspended over the flame. The lamp was yet another Eskimo device. Unlike the oil-burning lamp with which we are familiar, it resembled rather half of a double omelet-pan that hinges in the middle. When the well was filled with seal-oil, the wick of cotton-grass seeds arranged along the straight front edge emitted a continuous flame about one inch high. The warmth from the lamp partially melted the snow walls, and converted the little snow-hut into a dome of ice, solid enough to resist the weight of a man, and proof against the strongest gales.

To contend with a winter temperature ranging out of doors from zero to sixty below, and seldom more than twenty degrees above zero Fahrenheit, even inside the snow-huts, the Eskimo wore clothing made entirely of caribou and seal skins sewn together with thread of caribou sinew. Their neat, tailored costume differed entirely from the loose, ill-fitting robes of the Indians to the south of them. Both men and women wore a hooded shirt, trousers, fur stockings that lapped over or

Photo by D. Jenness.

AN ESKIMO SNOW-HUT WITH A WINDOW OF ICE

The owner's poles and harpoons are planted in the walls, and his sled, upturned and
raised on snow blocks, faces the entrance.

under the trousers, and seal-skin boots that were high for summer and low for winter. The shirt was a cutaway, something like a full-dress coat, but with a short tail also in front; the long tail at the back provided a cushion for the hunter as he sat hour after hour on the ice, often during blinding gales, crouching patiently over the seal-holes. The women's shirt had a larger hood and wider sleeves than the men's, and an extra piece inserted between the shoulders to allow room for their babies, whom they carried on their backs directly against their bodies. In some districts their stockings were also expanded at the top, resembling the high rubber boots worn by Canadian river-men. All the best hunters had ceremonial costumes which they wore for special occasions; and these the women embellished with narrow bands of differently-coloured skin or fur, inset with extremely fine stitching on various parts of the shirt and trousers. Both in designing and tailoring the costumes, they displayed quite as much originality and skill as our most exclusive tailors.

In spite of their inventive genius, and a

certain artistic talent, the social life of the
Eskimo at the time of their discovery was
perhaps more primitive than that of any
Indian tribe in the Dominion. They recognized no clans or stable bands, but gathered
into small scattered communities, each of them
from ten to twenty families that clung together
for a year or two, then dispersed to form new
groupings. Men whose force of character
and unusual ability gave them prestige in the
community wielded a certain amount of influence, but they were not chiefs, and possessed
no real authority over either their own or
neighbouring groups. Theft was practically
unknown, because there was little to steal.
When murder occurred, as it did occasionally,
the murderer escaped scot-free, unless the relatives of his victim were sufficiently numerous
to retaliate and keep up the blood-feud. But
the Eskimo were a singularly good-natured,
tolerant people, and discord was the exception
amongst them rather than the rule. Marriage
was unmarked by any ceremony, and either
wife or husband could dissolve it at will. Men
even exchanged wives temporarily, for friend-
ship between families was held in higher

esteem than faithfulness to the marriage tie. However, married people usually clung together after children were born, and treated each other with kindness and affection. Women had a well-recognized place in the community, and their children an unusually happy lot. If the Eskimo, like the Mackenzie Indians, had no scruples against killing girl babies or abandoning the aged and infirm, we must not judge them by our standards, but remember that they wandered incessantly over land and ice, broke camp in the coldest weather, and ate only at the end of a successful hunt, when there was food for their cooking pots and oil for their shallow soapstone lamps.

To alleviate the monotony of the long winter evenings, and of days so stormy that the hunters could not go to the sealing grounds, they had one distraction—singing and dancing to the beating of drums. Almost all their songs were dance-songs, and they seldom sang outside the dance-house, although sometimes a woman murmured a tune as she rocked her baby on her back, and a man lying sleepless in the darkness of his hut relieved the tedium

114

Photo by J. R. Cox.

COPPER ESKIMO WOMAN AND CHILD

of the night hours by singing. But whenever a few people gathered in the dance-house some one soon produced a drum, while the others ranged themselves in a circle around him and started a chorus. Hour after hour they stood in the ring, dancer succeeding dancer as each in turn became exhausted and dropped back to a place in the chorus. There were no harmonies in their songs; the men merely sang an octave lower than the women. Their scales, too, were different from those of European music, and the words influenced the metres much more than we allow. Yet some of their melodies were so beautiful that professional musicians have reproduced them occasionally on concert platforms in Europe and America.

Religion in one form or another has influenced the minds of every tribe and nation inhabiting the globe. To most it has brought comfort and hope; to a few, and among them the Eskimo, neither consolation nor cheer. They believed the world to be governed by supernatural beings of various shapes and forms, who controlled the supply of caribou and seals on which they relied for their daily

116

food. Most of these spirits were malevolent
and tried to injure them on every occasion;
happily, a few were more kindly and sometimes interceded in their favour to curb the
workings of the evil ones. Guardian spirits
existed, it was thought, but only to a few
chosen men and women would they reveal
themselves. Such favoured individuals became
medicine-men and medicine-women, who used
their powers to cure disease, to propitiate the
evil spirits and to foretell the future. The
souls of the dead, accounted benevolent by
most primitive tribes, also ranked as evil
beings that haunted their old homes on earth,
and sought to harm even their own kinsmen
and children. Yet, in spite of so gloomy an
outlook upon nature and her phenomena, the
Eskimo, unlike their Indian neighbors, were
one of the most laughter-loving people on
earth. Their invariable cheerfulness in the
face of every hardship shows that man can
rise above his surroundings, no matter how
harsh they may be, and find contentment even
in the most difficult circumstances of life.

Chapter IX

THE EFFECT OF CIVILIZATION

THE occupation of Canada by Europeans completely revolutionized the lives of the Indians. Whether they foresaw it or not, only two courses lay open to them, either to Europeanize themselves, to adopt all the customs and habits of the colonists, or to be pushed to one side and to eke out a precarious existence in the old way by fishing and hunting, wherever the new settlers left them room. Throughout the southern part of Canada the second alternative is no longer possible. The game is disappearing with the forests, which are being cut down for roads and railways, for farms and cities; and sheep and cattle pasture on the grazing grounds of the deer and moose. On the plains waving fields of wheat have superseded the countless herds of buffalo that the Indians once ran down on horseback or butchered in pounds. Even north of the railways, where European settlements are few and far between, firearms have seriously diminished the caribou and the musk-oxen, and intensive trapping by both whites and Indians has decreased the numbers of the beaver and other fur-bearing animals that kept the Indians prosperous in the early days of the fur trade. Conditions have changed completely, and they are still changing. The gasoline engine and the aeroplane are taking the prospector and the miner into the remotest fastnesses of the Indians, into the heart of Labrador and of the Barren Lands, and into the mountainous divide that separates the basin of the Mackenzie River from the Yukon. Before many years these northern Indians, too, will no longer be able to live by hunting and trapping alone, even though they avail themselves of civilization's latest inventions. During the 19th century nearly all the southern Indians were confined to reserves in order that settlement might proceed more rapidly; and it may be that the same method will be adopted for the northern Indians also. Yet, in the north as in the south, it can only be a temporary measure, to ease their transition from the old life to the life of the Europeans round them.

There is really no reason why the Indians

should not gain full citizenship, and share all the labours of the Europeans who have wrested the country from their hands. We may suspect certain peoples of being less intelligent than the average white man, but certainly our Indians are not inferior. In the past they made valuable contributions to the life of the early colonists. It was from the Indians that we learned to cultivate corn, beans, pumpkins, squashes and tobacco; indeed, all the varieties of corn we grow to-day were grown by the aborigines of America hundreds of years before Columbus. It was our Indians (and Eskimo) who taught the first settlers to make and use canoes, toboggans and the dog-sled, who guided them over the best trails and portages along routes that we follow to-day in our motor-cars and trains. Many of these settlers preferred Indian brides to girls of their own race, for ninety per cent. of the Indians, when dressed in European clothes, can mingle with Europeans unnoticed; and Indian blood has run in the veins of many men prominent in Canadian and United States history.

Contact with civilization did not bring

Photo by Harlan I. Smith.

THE TRANSFORMATION OF THE INDIAN—A CHILCOTIN COWBOY

unmeasured good to the Indians. It stopped the constant warfare between one tribe and another, and stamped out the killing of girl babies and the desertion of the aged and infirm. Yet it brought to them also terrible diseases, some of which still afflict their descendants to-day. The most terrible of all were the epidemics of smallpox that devastated wide areas in the 17th, 18th, and again in the 19th century, and destroyed probably half the population. Then there have been epidemics of typhus and of influenza that have killed off the Indians by hundreds. Tuberculosis has established itself in many regions, and is causing a high mortality, especially among the children and young people. All these diseases were unknown to the Indians in pre-European days. Unknown, too, was the spirituous liquor that the early fur-traders issued to them by the keg, until it undermined all their social and family life. This trade, fortunately, the government now prohibits, and exacts a heavy penalty from persons convicted of selling the Indians alcohol, or of letting it reach their hands.

In spite of all these evils, some tribes have